THE MAGICAL MIND: A KID'S GUIDE TO CBT AND MINDFULNESS

UNLOCKING THE POWER OF POSITIVE THINKING AND INNER PEACE

ALICE JENNIFER

CONTENTS

CHAPTER 1

THE MAGIC OF A HAPPY MIND: DISCOVERING CBT AND MINDFULNESS

Hello there, young readers! Are you ready to embark on a magical journey to a happier mind? In this chapter, we'll explore two incredible tools that can help you feel better and more joyful: CBT and mindfulness.

Now, you might be wondering, "What on earth are CBT and mindfulness?" Don't worry; we'll break it down for you in a way that's as easy as pie!

CBT stands for Cognitive Behavioral Therapy. It's a fancy term for a simple idea: the way we think and act can change the way we feel. Imagine you have a best friend who always looks on the bright side of life. They see the good in every situation, and their positive attitude is contagious. That's kind of like what CBT does for your brain – it helps you focus on the positive and feel better about yourself and the world around you.

For example, let's say you're having a tough day at school. Maybe you didn't do well on a test, or perhaps someone said something mean to you. It's easy to get caught up in negative thoughts like, "I'm not smart enough," or "Nobody likes me." But with CBT, you learn to challenge those negative thoughts and replace them with more positive ones. You might tell yourself, "I tried my best on that test, and I'll do better next time," or "That person's words don't define me. I know I'm a good friend." By changing your thoughts, you can change your feelings and feel happier overall.

Now, let's talk about mindfulness. Mindfulness is all about paying attention to the present moment without judgment. It means being aware of your thoughts, feelings, and surroundings in a gentle, curious way. When you're mindful, you're not worried about the past or anxious about the future. You're just enjoying the here and now.

One way to practice mindfulness is through breathing exercises. Take a moment right now to try it out. Find a comfortable spot to sit, and close your eyes. Take a deep breath in through your nose, filling up your belly like a balloon. Hold it for a second, then slowly breathe out through your mouth. Do this a few more times, focusing on the sensation of the air moving in and out of your body. If your mind starts to wander, that's okay! Just gently bring your attention back to your breath.

You can also practice mindfulness during everyday activities. When you're eating, take the time to appreciate the colors, smells, and flavors of your food. When you're walking, notice the feeling of your feet touching the ground and the sights and sounds around you. By being present and mindful, you can find joy and calm in even the simplest moments.

So, how can CBT and mindfulness help you feel happier? Let's explore some examples.

Imagine you're feeling anxious about an upcoming presentation at school. Using CBT, you can challenge the negative thoughts that are making you feel nervous. Instead of thinking, "I'm going to mess up and everyone will laugh at me," you can tell yourself, "I've prepared well for this presentation, and I'm going to do my best. Even if I make a mistake, it's not the end of the world." By reframing your thoughts, you can feel more confident and less anxious.

Now, let's say you're feeling overwhelmed by a busy schedule. Using mindfulness, you can take a moment to pause and breathe. Find a quiet spot, close your eyes, and focus on your breath. Notice any thoughts or feelings that come up, but don't judge them. Just let them pass by like clouds in the sky. By taking a mindful break, you can feel more centered and better able to handle the challenges of the day.

CBT and mindfulness can also help you cope with difficult emotions. Let's say you're feeling sad because your best friend is moving away. It's normal to feel upset when things change, but with CBT, you can learn to manage your emotions in a healthy way. You might tell yourself, "It's okay to feel sad, but I know I can still keep in touch with my friend through video chats and letters." You can also use mindfulness to comfort yourself. Take a moment to give yourself a big hug, or imagine a warm, soothing light surrounding you. By being kind and compassionate to yourself, you can weather even the toughest emotional storms.

As you can see, CBT and mindfulness are powerful tools that can help you feel happier, calmer, and more resilient. But the best part? Anyone can learn to use them, including you!

Here are a few simple ways to start incorporating CBT and mindfulness into your daily life:

1 Keep a positive thought diary. Every day, write down three good things that happened to you, no matter how small. This helps train your brain to focus on the positive.

2 Practice belly breathing. Whenever you feel anxious or upset, take a moment to do some deep belly breaths. This helps calm your body and mind.

3 Go on a mindful walk. Take a stroll around your neighborhood, paying attention to the sights, sounds, and sensations around you. Notice the feel of the sun on your skin, the chirping of the birds, and the rustling of the leaves.

4 Challenge negative self-talk. When you catch yourself thinking negative thoughts about yourself, ask, "Is this really true?" Look for evidence that proves those thoughts wrong, and replace them with kinder, more accurate ones.

5 Express gratitude. Every night before bed, think of three things you're grateful for. It could be a delicious meal, a fun game with friends, or a cozy hug from a loved one. Focusing on gratitude helps shift your mind to a more positive state.

Remember, learning CBT and mindfulness is like learning any new skill – it takes practice. Be patient and kind with yourself as you embark on this journey. Celebrate your successes, no matter how small, and don't beat yourself up if you have a tough day. With time and practice, you'll develop a toolbox of CBT and mindfulness techniques that you can use to navigate life's ups and downs with greater ease and joy.

In conclusion, CBT and mindfulness are like magic keys that can unlock the door to a happier, more peaceful mind. By learning to change your thoughts and stay present in the moment, you can transform your outlook on life and face challenges with resilience and grace. So, young readers, embrace the magic of a happy mind – the power is within you!

As we move forward in this book, we'll dive deeper into specific CBT and mindfulness techniques that you can use to manage anxiety, boost self-esteem, navigate friendships, and more. Get ready for an exciting adventure into the world of a happier, more mindful you!

CHAPTER 2

THE THOUGHT-FEELING CONNECTION: BECOMING FRIENDS WITH YOUR MIND

Welcome back, young explorers of the mind! In our last chapter, we discovered the magical world of CBT and mindfulness. Now, we're going to dive deeper into one of the most important parts of CBT: understanding the connection between your thoughts and your feelings.

Have you ever noticed how your thoughts can affect your mood? Maybe you wake up in the morning and think, "Today is going to be a great day!" Suddenly, you feel excited and energized, ready to take on the world. Or perhaps you're about to take a test, and you think, "I'm going to fail." All at once, you feel nervous and discouraged, like you want to hide under your desk.

This is the thought-feeling connection in action. Our thoughts have the power to shape our emotions, for better or for worse. But the good news is, we can learn to become friends with our minds and choose thoughts that help us feel happy and confident.

First, let's explore how thoughts and feelings are connected. Imagine your mind is like a garden. Your thoughts are the seeds you plant in the soil. If you plant seeds of positivity, like "I am capable" or "I am loved," you'll grow a garden of happy, healthy feelings. But if you plant seeds of negativity, like "I'm not good enough" or "Nobody likes me," you'll grow a garden of sad, anxious feelings.

Just like a real garden, your mind needs regular tending to stay healthy. This means paying attention to your thoughts and weeding out the negative ones before they take root. It also means nurturing the positive thoughts with plenty of self-love and encouragement.

Now, you might be thinking, "But I can't control my thoughts! They just pop into my head without warning." And you're right – thoughts can be sneaky like that. But with practice, you can learn to catch negative thoughts before they spiral out of control and replace them with more helpful ones.

Let's look at an example. Imagine you're playing soccer with your friends, and you miss an easy goal. A negative thought pops into your head: "I'm the worst player ever. I let my whole team down." Ouch! That thought doesn't feel good at all. But what if you could catch that thought and swap it for a more positive one? You might tell yourself, "Missing one goal doesn't define me as a player. I'll keep practicing and do better next time." Ah, that feels much better!

It takes practice to get good at catching and changing negative thoughts, but it's a skill that anyone can learn. Here are a few tips to get you started:

1 Be a thought detective. Start paying attention to the thoughts that run through your head. When you notice a negative thought, ask yourself, "Is this thought helping me or hurting me?"

2 Talk back to negative thoughts. When you catch a negative thought, don't just let it boss you around. Talk back to it with a more positive, helpful thought. For example, if you think, "I'm so bad at math," you could say, "Math is challenging for me, but I'm working hard and improving every day."

3 Give your positive thoughts a megaphone. Whenever you have a positive thought, give it some extra attention. Repeat it to yourself a few times, or write it down in a journal. The more you focus on positive thoughts, the stronger they'll become.

4 Practice self-compassion. Treat yourself with the same kindness and understanding you'd show a good friend. When you make a mistake or face a challenge, remind yourself that everyone struggles sometimes, and that you're doing your best.

Let's practice using these tips with a few more examples.

Example 1: You're invited to a birthday party, but you're nervous about meeting new people. A negative thought pops into your head: "I'm so awkward. No one will want to talk to me."

Thought detective: Is this thought helping or hurting? It's definitely hurting! It's making you feel anxious and insecure.

Talk back: "I may feel awkward at first, but I'm a friendly person with interesting things to say. People will enjoy getting to know me."

Give your positive thought a megaphone: Repeat to yourself, "I am friendly and interesting. People will enjoy talking to me."

Practice self-compassion: "It's normal to feel nervous in new situations. I'm brave for putting myself out there, and I'm proud of myself for trying."

Example 2: You're working on a school project, but you're having trouble coming up with ideas. A negative thought pops into your head: "I'm not creative. This project is going to be a disaster."

Thought detective: Is this thought helping or hurting? It's hurting! It's making you feel discouraged and stuck.

Talk back: "I may not have the perfect idea yet, but I'm a creative person with a good imagination. If I keep brainstorming, I'll come up with something great."

Give your positive thought a megaphone: Write down, "I am creative and imaginative. I have great ideas inside me."

Practice self-compassion: "It's okay to feel stuck sometimes. All creative people struggle with ideas at first. I'm doing my best, and I'll keep trying."

As you can see, becoming friends with your mind takes practice, but it's so worth it. When you learn to catch and change negative thoughts, you'll feel more confident, resilient, and in control of your emotions.

But what about those times when negative thoughts are really stubborn and won't go away? That's where mindfulness can help. Remember, mindfulness is all about paying attention to the present moment without judgment. When you're feeling overwhelmed by negative thoughts, take a mindful pause. Close your eyes, take a few deep breaths, and just notice your thoughts without getting caught up in them. Imagine they're like clouds floating by in the sky – you can see them, but you don't have to hold onto them.

Here's an example of how mindfulness can help with stubborn negative thoughts:

Example 3: You got into an argument with your sibling, and now you can't stop thinking about how angry and hurt you feel. The negative thoughts keep swirling around in your head: "They always treat me so unfairly. I can't stand it!"

Take a mindful pause: Find a quiet spot and sit down. Close your eyes and take a few deep, slow breaths.

Notice your thoughts: Without judging them as good or bad, just observe the thoughts that are running through your head. "I notice

I'm thinking about the argument with my sibling. I notice I'm feeling angry and hurt."

Let your thoughts pass by: Imagine your thoughts are like leaves floating down a stream. Watch them drift by without trying to hold onto them or push them away.

Return to the present moment: Bring your attention back to your breath, your body, and your surroundings. Notice the sensations of sitting, the sounds around you, the feel of the air on your skin.

By taking a mindful pause, you give yourself space to step back from negative thoughts and find a sense of calm and clarity. You may still feel upset about the argument, and that's okay. But by practicing mindfulness, you can learn to ride the waves of difficult emotions without getting pulled under.

As you continue to explore the thought-feeling connection and practice CBT and mindfulness techniques, remember to be patient and kind with yourself. Changing our thought patterns takes time, and there will be days when negative thoughts get the best of us. That's just part of being human.

But by learning to become friends with your mind – to notice your thoughts, challenge the negative ones, and cultivate positivity and self-compassion – you'll develop a superpower that will serve you well throughout your life. You'll be better equipped to handle life's challenges, bounce back from setbacks, and find joy and meaning in each day.

So keep exploring, keep practicing, and keep befriending your mind. The more you do, the more you'll discover just how strong, wise, and wonderful you truly are.

And remember, no matter what thoughts may be swirling around in your head, you are always deserving of love, happiness, and peace. Your thoughts do not define you – they're just passing clouds in the vast, beautiful sky of your mind.

Keep shining, young mind explorers! The world needs your light.

CHAPTER 3
THE HAPPY THOUGHT SUPERPOWER: UNLEASHING POSITIVE THINKING

Welcome back, young mind adventurers! In the last chapter, we explored the magical connection between your thoughts and your feelings. Now, it's time to dive into one of the most exciting parts of CBT: unleashing the superpower of positive thinking!

Imagine you could carry a special flashlight with you wherever you go. But instead of shining regular light, this flashlight would shine a beam of positivity, turning everything it touched into something bright and wonderful. Well, guess what? You already have this superpower inside you – it's called positive thinking!

Positive thinking means focusing on the good things in life, even when faced with challenges or setbacks. It's about choosing to see the best in yourself, others, and the world around you. And just like a muscle, the more you practice positive thinking, the stronger and more natural it becomes.

But why is positive thinking so important? Well, research shows that people who think positively tend to be happier, healthier, and more successful than those who dwell on negative thoughts. Positive thinkers are better at handling stress, bouncing back from disappointments, and finding creative solutions to problems.

On the other hand, negative thinking can be like a dark cloud that follows you around, raining on your parade and making everything seem gloomy and hopeless. Negative thoughts can zap your energy, dampen your mood, and hold you back from trying new things or believing in yourself.

So, how can you start flexing your positive thinking muscles? Here are a few simple tips:

1 Look for the good in every situation. Even when things don't go your way, try to find something positive to focus on. For

example, if you get a disappointing grade on a test, instead of thinking, "I'm a failure," try thinking, "This test was tough, but I learned a lot and I know I can do better next time."

2 Practice gratitude. Take time each day to think about the things you're thankful for, big and small. It could be a delicious breakfast, a kind word from a friend, or a beautiful sunset. The more you focus on gratitude, the more you'll train your brain to notice and appreciate the good things in life.

3 Surround yourself with positive people. Just like laughter, positivity is contagious! Seek out friends and family members who uplift and encourage you, and try to spend less time with people who bring you down or criticize you.

4 Use positive self-talk. The way you talk to yourself matters a lot. Instead of putting yourself down or dwelling on your mistakes, try using kind and encouraging words. For example, instead of thinking, "I'm so clumsy," try thinking, "I'm learning and growing every day."

5 Visualize success. Before tackling a big challenge or goal, take a few minutes to close your eyes and imagine yourself succeeding. Picture every detail, from how you'll feel to what you'll say and do. This kind of positive visualization can help you feel more confident and motivated.

Now, let's explore some examples of how positive thinking can help you in real life.

Example 1: You're trying out for the school play, but you're nervous about auditioning in front of everyone. Negative thoughts start creeping in: "I'm going to forget my lines. Everyone will laugh at me. I'm not good enough."

Positive thinking to the rescue! Instead of letting those negative thoughts take over, try shining your positivity flashlight on the situation. Think thoughts like, "I've practiced my lines and I know them well. I'm going to do my best and have fun. Even if I make a mistake, it's not the end of the world."

By focusing on the positive, you'll feel more confident and relaxed during your audition. And who knows – you might just land the starring role!

Example 2: You're having a hard time making friends at your new school. Negative thoughts keep popping up: "No one likes me. I'm too shy. I'll never fit in."

Time to unleash your positive thinking superpower! Instead of believing those negative thoughts, try thinking, "It takes time to make new friends. I'm a kind and interesting person, and I have a lot to offer. If I keep being friendly and joining in activities, I'll find my place here."

By shifting your focus to the positive, you'll feel more hopeful and motivated to keep putting yourself out there. And before you know it, you'll have a whole group of new friends who appreciate you for who you are.

Example 3: You're learning a new skill, like playing the piano, but you keep making mistakes. Negative thoughts start swirling: "I'm not musically talented. I'll never be good at this. I should just quit."

Positive thinking powers, activate! Instead of getting discouraged, try thinking, "Learning something new takes time and practice. Every mistake is a chance to learn and improve. If I keep at it, I'll get better and better."

By embracing a positive attitude, you'll be more resilient in the face of challenges and setbacks. You'll understand that mistakes are a normal part of the learning process, and you'll keep pushing yourself to grow and improve.

As you can see, positive thinking is a powerful tool that can help you in all areas of life. But it's important to remember that being positive doesn't mean ignoring your feelings or pretending everything is perfect all the time. It's okay to feel sad, angry, or scared sometimes – those feelings are just as valid and important as the happy ones.

The key is to acknowledge your difficult feelings without getting stuck in them. When you're feeling down, try using your positive thinking skills to find a silver lining or a way forward. For example, if you're feeling lonely, you might think, "I miss my friends, but this is a chance for me to reach out and connect with someone new."

It's also important to be realistic in your positive thinking. Telling yourself "I'm the best at everything!" or "Nothing bad will ever happen to me!" isn't helpful, because it sets you up for disappointment when reality doesn't match those high expectations. Instead, focus on thoughts that are hopeful but grounded in truth, like "I have strengths and weaknesses, and that's okay," or "I can handle whatever challenges come my way."

As you practice positive thinking, be patient and kind with yourself. Changing your thought patterns takes time and effort, and there will be days when negative thoughts get the best of you. That's just part of being human. The important thing is to keep coming back to your positive thinking superpower, again and again, until it becomes a natural part of who you are.

And remember, positive thinking isn't just about making yourself feel good – it's also about spreading light and joy to the people around you. When you choose to focus on the good, you become a force for positivity in the world. You inspire others to see the best in themselves and in life, and you help create a ripple effect of happiness and kindness.

So keep shining your positivity flashlight, young mind explorers. Keep looking for the good, practicing gratitude, surrounding yourself with uplifting people, using kind self-talk, and visualizing success. The more you flex your positive thinking muscles, the stronger and more resilient you'll become.

And always remember: you have the power to choose your thoughts, and your thoughts have the power to shape your reality. So choose wisely, and choose positively. The world needs your unique brand of magic and light.

Keep glowing, keep growing, and keep embracing the happy thought superpower within you. With a positive mindset, there's no limit to the amazing things you can achieve and the wonderful life you can create.

Onward and upward, young mind adventurers! The best is yet to come.

CHAPTER 4

MINDFUL BREATHING ADVENTURES: FINDING CALM AND RELAXATION

Hello again, brave explorers of the mind! In the last chapter, we discovered the incredible superpower of positive thinking. Now, it's time to embark on a new adventure – the wonderful world of mindful breathing!

Have you ever noticed how your breath is always with you, no matter where you go or what you do? It's like a faithful friend, constantly by your side. But did you know that your breath can also be a powerful tool for finding calm and relaxation?

Mindful breathing is all about paying attention to your breath in a gentle, curious way. It's about taking a break from the busy world around you and turning your focus inward, to the simple but amazing process of breathing in and breathing out.

When you practice mindful breathing, you're giving your mind and body a chance to rest and recharge. You're hitting the "pause" button on stress, worry, and overthinking, and allowing yourself to just be in the present moment.

Think of it like taking a mini-vacation for your mind. Just like you might go to the beach or the mountains to relax and unwind, mindful breathing is a way to find peace and calm right where you are, anytime you need it.

So, how exactly do you practice mindful breathing? It's easier than you might think! Here's a simple step-by-step guide:

1 Find a quiet, comfortable place to sit or lie down. This could be on a cushion, a chair, or even your bed.

2 Close your eyes and take a few moments to settle in. Notice how your body feels – the weight of your limbs, the temperature of the air on your skin, any sensations of tension or relaxation.

3 Begin to focus on your breath. Don't try to change it or control it – just notice it, as it is. Feel the air moving in through your nose or mouth, filling up your lungs, and then flowing back out again.

4 If your mind starts to wander (and it probably will – that's normal!), gently redirect your attention back to your breath. You might silently say to yourself, "breathing in, breathing out" to help you stay focused.

5 Keep breathing and noticing for as long as you like – even just a few minutes can make a big difference in how you feel.

That's it! With regular practice, mindful breathing can become a valuable tool in your self-care toolkit, helping you find calm and balance in the midst of life's ups and downs.

But don't just take my word for it – let's explore some real-life examples of how mindful breathing can help!

Example 1: Imagine you're about to give a presentation in front of your whole class. Your heart is racing, your palms are sweaty, and your mind is filled with worried thoughts. "What if I mess up? What if everyone laughs at me?"

This is the perfect time for some mindful breathing! Before you start your presentation, take a few moments to close your eyes and focus on your breath. Inhale deeply, feeling your belly expand like a balloon. Exhale slowly, letting all the air whoosh out. Repeat this a few times, until you feel your body start to relax and your mind start to clear.

By taking this mindful breathing break, you're giving yourself a chance to calm your nerves and refocus your energy. You're reminding yourself that you're capable and prepared, and that you've got this! And when you step up to give your presentation, you'll feel more grounded, confident, and ready to shine.

Example 2: Let's say you're having trouble falling asleep at night. Your mind is buzzing with thoughts about the day, the week, the future. You toss and turn, trying to get comfortable, but sleep just won't come.

Enter mindful breathing! Instead of getting frustrated or anxious, try focusing on your breath as you lie in bed. Take a slow, deep inhale through your nose, counting silently to four. Hold the breath for a moment, then exhale slowly through your mouth, counting to six. Repeat this pattern, making your exhales a bit longer than your inhales.

As you breathe, imagine each exhale is carrying away your worries and tension, like leaves floating down a stream. Each inhale brings in fresh, peaceful energy, filling you up with calm and relaxation. With every breath, feel your body sinking deeper into your bed, your mind growing quieter and more still.

By using mindful breathing as a bedtime ritual, you're signaling to your mind and body that it's time to rest and let go. You're creating a sense of safety and comfort, inviting sleep to come naturally and gently. And even if you don't fall asleep right away, you're still giving yourself the gift of a few precious moments of peace and stillness.

Example 3: Picture this – you're in the middle of a heated argument with a friend or family member. Tempers are flaring, voices are rising, and you can feel your anger and frustration building up inside you. You're about to say something you might regret, or storm off in a huff.

But wait – let's hit the pause button and try some mindful breathing instead! Even in the heat of the moment, you can take a few deep breaths to calm yourself down and clear your head. Inhale slowly through your nose, counting to five. Hold the breath for a moment, then exhale slowly through your mouth, counting to seven. Repeat a few times, focusing on the sensation of the air moving in and out of your body.

As you breathe, notice how your anger starts to dissipate, like a fire dying down to embers. Your mind begins to quiet, your perspective starts to shift. You might realize that the argument isn't worth losing your cool over, or that there's a better way to communicate your feelings.

By using mindful breathing as a tool for emotional regulation, you're giving yourself the space to respond rather than react. You're choosing to approach the situation with a clearer, calmer mind, and a more open heart. And who knows – you might even be able to find a resolution or compromise that works for everyone.

As you can see, mindful breathing is a simple but powerful practice that can help you in all kinds of situations – from easing stress and anxiety to improving sleep to navigating difficult emotions and relationships.

And the best part? You can practice mindful breathing anytime, anywhere – no special equipment or skills required! All you need is your breath and a willingness to pay attention to it.

Of course, like any new skill, mindful breathing takes practice. At first, you might find it hard to stay focused on your breath, or to quiet your busy mind. That's totally normal! Remember, the goal isn't to stop your thoughts completely, but rather to notice them without getting too caught up in them.

One helpful tip is to imagine your thoughts as clouds drifting across the sky of your mind. When you notice a thought, simply acknowledge it, then gently redirect your attention back to your breath. You might even say to yourself, "thinking" or "wandering" as a way of labeling the thought before letting it go.

Another tip is to experiment with different types of mindful breathing to find what works best for you. Some people like to count their breaths, while others prefer to focus on the sensation of the air moving in and out of their nostrils. You might try visualizing your breath as a color or a shape, or even imagining it as a soothing, healing energy filling up your body.

The key is to approach mindful breathing with a sense of curiosity and playfulness, rather than trying to force it or do it "perfectly." Remember, there's no right or wrong way to breathe mindfully – the most important thing is to keep showing up and giving it your best shot.

And as you continue to practice mindful breathing, you might start to notice some pretty amazing benefits. You might feel less stressed and anxious overall, and more able to handle life's challenges with grace and resilience. You might sleep better, feel more focused and productive, and even experience a greater sense of joy and contentment in your daily life.

But perhaps the greatest gift of mindful breathing is the way it connects you to the present moment – the only moment we ever really have. When you're fully absorbed in your breath, you're not worrying about the future or dwelling on the past. You're right here, right now, alive and aware and whole.

And that, my friends, is a true adventure – an adventure into the vast, mysterious, and endlessly fascinating landscape of your own mind and body. An adventure that requires no special equipment or destination, only a willingness to show up, pay attention, and breathe.

So take a deep breath, intrepid explorers. Close your eyes, feel the air flowing in and out, and let yourself be carried on the gentle waves of your own breathing. Trust that in this moment, you are exactly where you need to be, and that your breath will always be there to guide you home.

Keep breathing, keep exploring, and keep discovering the magic and wonder that lies within you. The adventure of mindfulness is just beginning!

CHAPTER 5

EVERYDAY MINDFULNESS MAGIC: ENJOYING THE PRESENT MOMENT

Welcome back, mindful adventurers! In the last chapter, we dove deep into the world of mindful breathing and discovered how this simple yet powerful practice can help us find calm and relaxation in the midst of life's ups and downs.

Now, it's time to expand our mindfulness journey beyond the breath and into the magic of everyday moments. That's right – mindfulness isn't just something we practice on a cushion or a yoga mat. It's a way of living, a way of being present and awake to the wonders and joys that surround us all the time, if only we pay attention.

Think of it like this: every moment of our lives is a precious gift, a once-in-a-lifetime opportunity to experience something new and amazing. But how often do we rush through our days, lost in thoughts about the past or worries about the future, missing out on the beauty and richness that's right in front of us?

That's where everyday mindfulness comes in. By bringing our full attention to the present moment, we can start to savor and appreciate all the little things that make life so sweet – the warmth of the sun on our skin, the laughter of a friend, the taste of a juicy apple, the feeling of accomplishment after a job well done.

Mindfulness is like a magic magnifying glass that helps us see the world with fresh eyes, as if for the first time. It's a way of waking up to the wonder and awe that's always available to us, if only we remember to look.

So, how can we start bringing more mindfulness into our daily lives? Here are a few simple tips and practices to get you started:

1 Mindful Eating: Next time you sit down for a meal or a snack, try slowing down and paying full attention to the experience. Notice the colors, shapes, and textures of the food on your plate. Take a moment to appreciate the aroma and anticipate the flavors. As you

eat, really savor each bite, noticing the taste, temperature, and sensations in your mouth and body. You might be surprised at how much more enjoyable and satisfying your food becomes when you eat with mindfulness!

2 Mindful Walking: Take a break from your busy day and go for a mindful walk, even if it's just around the block. As you walk, pay attention to the sensations of your feet touching the ground, the movement of your legs and arms, the rhythm of your breath. Notice the sights, sounds, and smells around you – the chirping of birds, the rustling of leaves, the colorful flowers or interesting architecture. Allow yourself to be fully present in the moment, letting go of any thoughts or worries and just enjoying the simple pleasure of walking.

3 Mindful Listening: When you're in conversation with someone, practice mindful listening by giving them your full, undivided attention. Put away any distractions like your phone or computer, and really tune in to what the other person is saying. Notice their facial expressions, body language, and tone of voice. Listen not just to respond, but to understand and empathize. You might be amazed at how much deeper and more meaningful your interactions become when you listen with mindfulness.

4 Mindful Breathing Breaks: Throughout your day, take short mindful breathing breaks to reconnect with the present moment and recharge your batteries. You can do this anytime, anywhere – at your desk, in the car, while waiting in line. Simply close your eyes, take a few deep breaths, and focus on the sensations of the air moving in and out of your body. Notice any thoughts or feelings that arise, then gently redirect your attention back to your breath. Even just a minute or two of mindful breathing can help you feel more centered, calm, and focused.

These are just a few examples of how you can start incorporating mindfulness into your everyday life. The possibilities are truly endless! You can bring mindfulness to any activity, from brushing your teeth to doing the dishes to playing with your pet. The key is to approach each moment with curiosity, openness, and a willingness to be fully present.

Now, let's explore some real-life examples of how everyday mindfulness can make a big difference in our lives:

Example 1: Sarah loves to paint, but lately she's been feeling stuck and uninspired. She sits down at her easel, but her mind is full of worries and doubts. "What if I mess up? What if my painting isn't good enough?"

Then Sarah remembers her mindfulness practice. She takes a deep breath and focuses on the present moment. She notices the feel of the paintbrush in her hand, the bright colors on her palette, the blank canvas waiting to be filled. She allows herself to get lost in the process, letting go of any expectations or judgments and just enjoying the act of creating.

As Sarah paints, she feels a sense of joy and freedom bubbling up inside her. She's not thinking about the final product or what anyone else will think. She's simply savoring the moment, the flow of creativity, the magic of making something new.

By bringing mindfulness to her painting practice, Sarah rediscovers her love and passion for art. She learns to trust her intuition, to take risks and experiment, to embrace imperfection and find beauty in the journey. And when she steps back from her finished painting, she feels a deep sense of satisfaction and pride, knowing that she poured her heart and soul into every brushstroke.

Example 2: Jack is a busy college student, always rushing from one class to the next, trying to juggle homework, extracurriculars, and a part-time job. He often feels overwhelmed and stressed out, like he's never doing enough or achieving enough.

One day, Jack decides to try a mindful walking practice. He leaves his dorm room and heads outside, taking a slow, deliberate walk around campus. At first, his mind is racing with thoughts and worries, but as he focuses on the sensations of walking, he starts to feel more grounded and present.

Jack notices the crunch of leaves underfoot, the cool breeze on his face, the dappled sunlight filtering through the trees. He sees the smiles on the faces of passing students, hears the laughter and chatter of friends enjoying a game of frisbee on the quad. He feels a sense of connection and belonging, like he's part of something bigger than himself.

As Jack continues his mindful walk, he starts to gain a new perspective on his life. He realizes that he doesn't have to be perfect or do everything. He can take things one step at a time, one moment at a time, and trust that he's doing his best. He feels a sense of gratitude for all the opportunities and experiences he's had, and a renewed sense of purpose and motivation.

By making mindful walking a regular part of his routine, Jack learns to manage his stress and anxiety, to prioritize his well-being, and to find joy and meaning in the present moment. He discovers that mindfulness is not just a practice, but a way of living – a way of showing up fully and authentically for himself and others.

Example 3: Emily is a mom of two young kids, and she often feels like she's running on empty. Between the constant demands of parenting, household chores, and work, she rarely has a moment to herself. She loves her family deeply, but sometimes she feels like she's losing touch with who she is and what matters most to her.

One evening, after a particularly challenging day, Emily decides to try a mindful breathing practice before bed. She sits down on the edge of her bed, closes her eyes, and takes a few deep breaths. At first, her mind is full of the day's stresses and worries, but as she focuses on the sensation of breathing, she starts to feel more calm and centered.

Emily notices the weight of her body sinking into the bed, the gentle rise and fall of her chest, the cool air entering her nostrils and the warm air leaving her mouth. She imagines each breath as a wave, washing away any tension or negativity and bringing in fresh, positive energy.

As Emily continues to breathe mindfully, she feels a sense of peace and clarity wash over her. She remembers what's truly important – her love for her family, her own health and happiness, her dreams and aspirations. She feels a renewed sense of strength and resilience, knowing that she can handle whatever challenges come her way.

By making mindful breathing a daily practice, Emily learns to carve out moments of self-care and self-compassion, even in the midst of a busy and demanding life. She discovers that mindfulness is not about escaping her reality, but about showing up for it with greater presence, patience, and love. She becomes a more grounded and joyful parent, partner, and person, and inspires her family to embrace mindfulness as well.

As you can see, everyday mindfulness has the power to transform our lives in countless ways, big and small. It can help us find calm in the chaos, joy in the ordinary, connection in the midst of isolation, and meaning in the face of adversity.

But mindfulness is not a quick fix or a magic cure-all. It's a lifelong journey, a daily practice, a way of being in the world that requires patience, persistence, and a willingness to show up again and again, even when it's hard.

There will be days when your mind is too busy or your heart is too heavy to be mindful. There will be moments when you forget to pay attention, when you get caught up in old patterns and habits, when you feel like giving up.

That's okay. Mindfulness is not about perfection, but about progress. It's about learning to be kind and compassionate with ourselves, to forgive our mistakes and start again, to trust in the power of the present moment to heal and transform us.

So keep practicing, mindful adventurers. Keep breathing, keep noticing, keep savoring the magic of everyday moments. Keep showing up for yourselves and each other with curiosity, openness, and love.

And remember, every moment is a new beginning, a fresh start, an opportunity to be fully alive and awake to the wonders of this precious life. All we have to do is pay attention, and the magic will reveal itself.

Happy mindful living, my friends! May your days be filled with presence, joy, and endless adventures in the extraordinary ordinary.

CHAPTER 6

THE BRAVE EXPLORER: CONQUERING FEARS AND WORRIES

Hello again, courageous adventurers! In the last chapter, we discovered the magic of everyday mindfulness and how it can help us find joy, calm, and connection in the present moment.

Now, we're going to embark on a new adventure – one that takes us deep into the heart of our fears and worries, and teaches us how to face them with bravery, resilience, and even a little bit of humor.

Let's face it – life can be scary sometimes. We all have fears and worries that keep us up at night, that make us feel small and vulnerable, that hold us back from going after our dreams and living our best lives.

Maybe you're afraid of the dark, or of speaking in front of your class, or of trying something new and failing. Maybe you worry about fitting in at school, or about your family's health and safety, or about the future of our planet.

These fears and worries are totally normal – in fact, they're a sign that you're human, that you care deeply about yourself and others, that you have a vivid imagination and a sensitive heart.

But here's the thing – your fears and worries don't have to control you. You have the power to face them, to learn from them, to use them as fuel for your growth and transformation.

That's where CBT comes in – remember, that stands for Cognitive Behavioral Therapy. It's a fancy way of saying that our thoughts, feelings, and actions are all connected, and that by changing one, we can change the others.

When it comes to conquering fears and worries, CBT gives us some powerful tools and strategies. Let's explore a few of them together:

1 Name Your Fears: The first step in facing your fears is to get to know them better. Give your fears and worries a name, like "The Worry Monster" or "The Fear Fairy." Draw a picture of what they

look like, or write a story about their adventures. By personifying your fears, you can start to see them as separate from yourself – as visitors in your mind, rather than who you are.

Example: Let's say you're afraid of dogs. You might imagine your fear as a yappy little Chihuahua named "Barky." Whenever Barky starts barking in your mind, you can say, "Oh, there goes Barky again! He's just trying to protect me, but I know I'm safe. I can handle this."

2 Challenge Your Thoughts: Our fears and worries often come from negative or irrational thoughts – thoughts that are based on worst-case scenarios, or that don't have much evidence to support them. CBT teaches us to challenge these thoughts, to question their validity, and to come up with more balanced and realistic alternatives.

Example: Let's say you're worried about an upcoming test. Your worry thoughts might sound like, "I'm going to fail this test. I'm not smart enough. I'll never get into college." But are those thoughts really true? Is there evidence to support them? You can challenge them by saying, "I've studied hard for this test. I've done well on tests before. Even if I don't get a perfect score, it's not the end of the world. I can always improve and try again."

3 Face Your Fears Gradually: When we're afraid of something, our natural instinct is to avoid it. But avoidance only makes our fears stronger over time. CBT encourages us to face our fears gradually, one small step at a time, until we build up our confidence and resilience.

Example: Let's say you're afraid of public speaking. Instead of avoiding it altogether, you can start by practicing in front of a mirror, then in front of a trusted friend or family member, then in front of a small group, and so on. Each time you face your fear, you'll feel a little braver and more capable, until eventually, public speaking becomes no big deal.

4 Use Positive Self-Talk: Our inner voice – the way we talk to ourselves in our minds – has a huge impact on how we feel and behave. If we're constantly telling ourselves that we're not good enough, that we can't handle challenges, that we're doomed to fail, then we'll start to believe it. But if we use positive self-talk – if we speak to ourselves with kindness, encouragement, and confidence – then we can start to see ourselves in a whole new light.

Example: Let's say you're worried about a big soccer game. Instead of telling yourself, "I'm going to mess up. I'm the worst player on the team," you can say, "I've practiced hard. I have skills and strengths. I'm going to give it my all and have fun, no matter what happens."

5 Practice Mindfulness: As we learned in the last chapter, mindfulness is a powerful tool for managing stress, anxiety, and difficult emotions. When we're feeling overwhelmed by fears and worries, we can use mindfulness to ground ourselves in the present moment, to find a sense of calm and clarity, and to gain perspective on our thoughts and feelings.

Example: Let's say you're feeling anxious about a family vacation. Your mind is racing with worries about the plane ride, the new place, the unfamiliar foods. You can practice mindfulness by taking a few deep breaths, noticing your surroundings, and focusing on your senses. You might say to yourself, "I'm feeling anxious, but that's okay. It's just a feeling, and it will pass. Right now, I'm safe and loved and capable of handling whatever comes my way."

These are just a few examples of how CBT and mindfulness can help us conquer our fears and worries. But the most important thing to remember is that bravery isn't about never feeling afraid – it's about feeling afraid and doing it anyway.

Bravery is about being honest with ourselves and others about our fears and worries, and seeking support and guidance when we need it.

Bravery is about taking small, steady steps towards our goals and dreams, even when the path is rocky and the destination is uncertain.

Bravery is about being kind and compassionate with ourselves when we stumble or fall, and getting back up again with a smile and a sense of humor.

Bravery is about embracing our uniqueness, our weirdness, our imperfections, and knowing that they make us beautiful and strong and one-of-a-kind.

So, my brave explorers, are you ready to face your fears and worries with courage and curiosity? Are you ready to go on an adventure into the uncharted territories of your mind and heart?

Great! Let's start by thinking of a fear or worry that's been on your mind lately. It could be something big or small, something specific or general, something real or imagined.

Now, let's give that fear or worry a name and a character. What does it look like? What does it sound like? What does it want from you?

Next, let's challenge some of the thoughts and beliefs that are fueling that fear or worry. Are they really true? Are they helpful or hurtful? What would a wise and loving friend say to you about them?

Now, let's come up with a small, manageable step you can take to face that fear or worry head-on. It could be something as simple as writing about it in a journal, talking to a trusted adult, or doing something that scares you (safely and responsibly, of course).

And finally, let's practice some mindfulness and self-compassion. Take a few deep breaths, put your hand on your heart, and repeat after me:

"I am brave. I am strong. I am capable of facing my fears and worries with kindness and courage. I am not alone, and I am loved just as I am."

Feel free to come up with your own affirmation or mantra – something that feels true and empowering to you.

And remember, my brave explorers, that conquering fears and worries is a lifelong journey, not a one-time event. There will be ups and downs, twists and turns, moments of triumph and moments of struggle.

But with each step you take, each fear you face, each worry you challenge, you'll grow stronger, wiser, and more resilient. You'll discover new parts of yourself, new sources of joy and meaning, new ways of connecting with others and the world around you.

So keep exploring, keep learning, keep growing. Keep being curious and compassionate with yourself and others. Keep seeking out stories, role models, and experiences that inspire you to be your bravest, most authentic self.

And know that wherever your adventures take you, you have everything you need inside you to handle whatever comes your way.

You are the hero of your own story, the brave explorer of your own mind and heart.

And I'm so excited to see where your courage and curiosity will lead you next.

Until then, happy adventuring! May your fears and worries be your teachers, your challenges be your opportunities, and your bravery be your superpower.

And may you always remember that you are braver than you think, stronger than you seem, and smarter than you believe.

CHAPTER 7

THE SELF-KINDNESS SUPERSTAR: TREATING YOURSELF WITH LOVE AND CARE

Hello again, my wonderful friends! In the last chapter, we learned how to be brave explorers, facing our fears and worries with courage and curiosity. We discovered that we have the power to challenge negative thoughts, take small steps towards our goals, and use mindfulness and self-compassion to support ourselves along the way.

Now, we're going to dive deeper into the topic of self-compassion and explore what it means to be a self-kindness superstar! Are you ready to learn how to treat yourself with the love and care you deserve? Let's go!

First, let's talk about what self-kindness really means. It's not about being selfish or self-centered. It's not about thinking you're better than anyone else or deserving special treatment. Instead, self-kindness is about treating yourself with the same warmth, understanding, and respect that you would offer to a good friend or a loved one.

Think about it – when a friend comes to you with a problem or a mistake they've made, do you criticize them harshly, or do you listen with empathy and offer words of encouragement? When a loved one is going through a tough time, do you judge them or blame them, or do you show them compassion and support?

Most likely, you're kind and caring towards the people you love – and that's wonderful! But do you extend that same kindness and care towards yourself?

Many of us are much harder on ourselves than we are on others. We have high expectations, we beat ourselves up for our flaws and failures, we compare ourselves unfavorably to others, and we neglect our own needs and feelings in the process.

But here's the thing – being kind to yourself isn't just a nice thing to do. It's essential for your mental health, your well-being, and your ability to thrive in life.

Research shows that self-compassion is strongly linked to happiness, resilience, and overall life satisfaction. People who are kind to themselves tend to have better relationships, cope better with stress and setbacks, and are more motivated to pursue their goals and dreams.

On the other hand, being harsh and critical towards yourself can lead to anxiety, depression, low self-esteem, and a host of other mental health challenges.

So, how can you start being a self-kindness superstar? Here are some tips and examples to get you started:

1 Treat yourself like a good friend. The next time you're feeling down on yourself or struggling with a challenge, imagine that you're talking to a good friend instead. What would you say to them? How would you support and encourage them? Now, try saying those same things to yourself. Example: Let's say you made a mistake on a test and you're feeling really upset about it. Instead of telling yourself "I'm so stupid. I'll never be good at this subject," try saying "It's okay. Everyone makes mistakes sometimes. I'll learn from this and do better next time. I believe in myself and my ability to improve."

2 Practice self-care. Taking care of yourself isn't selfish – it's necessary for your physical, emotional, and mental well-being. Make time for activities that make you feel good, like reading a book, taking a bath, going for a walk in nature, or spending time with loved ones. Example: Let's say you've been really busy with school and activities lately, and you're feeling exhausted and overwhelmed. Instead of pushing yourself to keep going, take a step back and ask yourself what you need. Maybe you need a quiet evening at home to rest and recharge. Maybe you need to say no to some commitments and prioritize your own needs. Remember – you can't pour from an empty cup!

3 Celebrate your strengths and accomplishments. We often focus on our weaknesses and failures, but it's just as important to acknowledge and celebrate our strengths and successes – no matter how small they may seem. Example: Let's say you finally worked up the courage to raise your hand in class and share your idea, even though you were nervous about speaking up. That's a big

accomplishment! Take a moment to feel proud of yourself and savor the positive feelings. You might even write it down in a journal or share it with a friend or family member.

4 Be mindful of your self-talk. The way you talk to yourself in your own mind has a powerful impact on your emotions and beliefs. Notice when you're engaging in negative self-talk, and try to reframe your thoughts in a more positive, supportive way. Example: Let's say you're getting ready for a big game or performance, and you catch yourself thinking "I'm not good enough. I'm going to mess up and let everyone down." Instead, try saying "I've worked hard and prepared for this. I'm going to do my best and have fun, no matter what happens. I am enough, just as I am."

5 Practice gratitude. Focusing on the things you're grateful for – big and small – can help shift your mindset from one of lack and negativity to one of abundance and appreciation. Make it a daily habit to think of a few things you're thankful for, and watch how it transforms your outlook on life. Example: Let's say you're having a rough day and everything seems to be going wrong. Take a moment to pause and think of a few things you're grateful for – perhaps a warm bed to sleep in, a delicious meal, a kind word from a friend, or a beautiful sunset. Savor those feelings of gratitude and let them fill you up from the inside out.

These are just a few examples of how you can start being a self-kindness superstar. But the most important thing is to find what works for you and make it a regular practice. Like any skill, self-compassion takes time and effort to develop – but the benefits are so worth it!

Now, I know what some of you might be thinking – "But isn't being kind to myself just letting myself off the hook? Won't I become lazy or complacent if I'm not hard on myself?"

The answer is a resounding no! In fact, research shows that self-compassion is actually a powerful motivator for growth and change. When we treat ourselves with kindness and understanding, we create a safe and supportive environment for learning, taking risks, and bouncing back from setbacks.

Think about it – when you're harsh and critical towards yourself, how does that make you feel? Probably pretty lousy, right? And when you're feeling lousy, are you more likely to take positive action or just want to give up and hide?

On the other hand, when you treat yourself with compassion and encouragement, you'll feel more confident, motivated, and resilient in the face of challenges. You'll be more likely to take healthy risks, learn from your mistakes, and keep going even when things get tough.

So, my dear self-kindness superstars, I invite you to make a commitment to treating yourself with love and care – not just today, but every day. Start small, be patient with yourself, and celebrate your progress along the way.

And remember – being kind to yourself isn't just a nice thing to do. It's a radical act of self-love and self-acceptance. It's a way of saying "I am worthy of compassion and respect, just as I am. I am enough, and I am deserving of love and care."

So go out there and spread that self-kindness magic! Be a role model for others, especially those who may be struggling with self-doubt or self-criticism. Show them that it's possible to be kind and supportive towards oneself, and watch how it transforms their lives too.

And don't forget to lean on your support system – your friends, family, teachers, and loved ones who believe in you and want to see you thrive. Surround yourself with people who uplift and inspire you, and who remind you of your inherent worth and goodness.

Because at the end of the day, being a self-kindness superstar isn't about being perfect or having it all figured out. It's about being human – flawed, messy, beautiful, and worthy of love and compassion, just as you are.

So keep shining your light, my friends. Keep spreading that self-kindness magic wherever you go. And know that you are never alone on this journey – we're all in this together, learning and growing and cheering each other on.

Here's to a lifetime of self-love, self-care, and self-compassion. May you always remember how amazing and deserving you truly are.

CHAPTER 8

THE FEELINGS FRIENDSHIP CLUB: EMBRACING AND UNDERSTANDING EMOTIONS

Hey there, my fantastic friends! In the last chapter, we learned all about becoming self-kindness superstars and treating ourselves with love and care. Now, get ready to dive into the exciting world of emotions and join The Feelings Friendship Club!

Have you ever felt like your feelings were a bit like a rollercoaster ride? One moment you're feeling happy and excited, and the next moment you might feel sad or angry. Well, guess what? That's totally normal! Emotions are a natural and important part of being human.

But sometimes, our emotions can feel a bit overwhelming or confusing. We might not know how to express them or deal with them in a healthy way. That's where The Feelings Friendship Club comes in!

In this club, we're all about embracing and understanding our emotions. We believe that all feelings are valid and deserve to be acknowledged and respected. And the best part? We're going to learn some super fun and easy ways to become friends with our feelings!

First things first, let's talk about what emotions actually are. Emotions are like messages from our brain and body that tell us how we're experiencing the world around us. They can be triggered by all sorts of things – a happy memory, a scary situation, or even a funny joke.

There are lots of different emotions out there, but some of the most common ones are:

1 Happiness – when we feel joyful, excited, or content.
2 Sadness – when we feel down, lonely, or disappointed.

3 Anger – when we feel frustrated, irritated, or mad.

4 Fear – when we feel scared, anxious, or worried.

5 Disgust – when we feel grossed out or uncomfortable.

6 Surprise – when something unexpected or shocking happens.

Now, here's the thing – all of these emotions are totally normal and okay to feel! There's no such thing as a "bad" emotion. They all serve a purpose and give us important information about ourselves and the world around us.

For example, let's say you're feeling really angry because your sibling borrowed your favorite toy without asking. That anger is telling you that something important to you has been crossed or disrespected. It's a sign that you need to communicate your boundaries and find a solution.

Or maybe you're feeling sad because your best friend is moving away. That sadness is a reflection of how much you care about your friend and how much you'll miss them. It's a way of honoring the special bond you share.

So, how can we start becoming friends with our feelings? Here are some fun activities to try:

1 Make a feelings collage. Grab some magazines, scissors, and glue, and create a collage that represents different emotions. You can cut out pictures, words, or colors that remind you of each feeling. Then, hang your collage somewhere you'll see it often as a reminder to embrace and understand your emotions.

2 Have a feelings dance party. Put on your favorite tunes and let your body express how you're feeling through dance! You can choose songs that match your current mood or experiment with different styles of music to see how they affect your emotions. Dancing is a great way to release pent-up feelings and boost your mood.

3 Keep a feelings journal. Writing about your emotions can be a powerful way to process and understand them. Each day, take a few minutes to jot down how you're feeling and why. You can also write about any thoughts or experiences that are connected to your emotions. Over time, you'll start to see patterns and gain insights into your emotional world.

4 Play feelings charades. Gather some friends or family members and take turns acting out different emotions without using any words. See if the others can guess what feeling you're expressing

based on your facial expressions and body language. This is a fun way to practice identifying and communicating emotions.

5 Create a feelings toolkit. Just like we talked about in the last chapter, having a self-care toolkit can be super helpful for managing emotions. But why not make a specific feelings toolkit too? Fill a box or bag with items that help you express and cope with different emotions. For example, you might include a stress ball for when you're feeling angry, a cozy blanket for when you're feeling sad, or a funny book for when you need a mood boost. Having these tools on hand can make it easier to navigate tough emotions in the moment.

Now, I know what some of you might be thinking – "But what if I don't want to feel certain emotions? What if I just want to be happy all the time?"

It's totally understandable to want to avoid uncomfortable or painful feelings. But the truth is, trying to push away or ignore our emotions usually just makes them feel bigger and scarier. It's like trying to hold a beach ball underwater – the harder you push down, the more forcefully it'll pop back up!

Instead, the key is to learn how to ride the waves of our emotions with curiosity and compassion. When we give ourselves permission to feel all our feelings, without judgment or resistance, they tend to naturally come and go more easily.

And here's the really cool part – by embracing and understanding our own emotions, we also become better at empathizing with and supporting others. We can create a ripple effect of emotional intelligence and kindness that makes the world a bit brighter for everyone.

So, are you ready to join The Feelings Friendship Club? Get ready to explore the wonderful world of emotions and discover just how awesome it can be to befriend your feelings!

Remember, all your feelings are valid and valuable. They're like colorful threads in the tapestry of your life, each one adding richness and depth to your story.

So, the next time you feel a big emotion bubbling up, try greeting it like an old friend. Say something like, "Hey there, [emotion]! I see you and I'm here to listen. What do you need from me right now?"

Then, use some of the fun activities we talked about to express and explore that emotion in a healthy way. You might be surprised at how much lighter and more peaceful you feel afterwards.

And don't forget to share your emotional adventures with your fellow Feelings Friendship Club members! We're all in this together, learning and growing and supporting each other along the way.

So, here's to a lifetime of emotional exploration, self-discovery, and big, beautiful feelings! May you always remember that your emotions are a gift, a compass, and a source of incredible strength and   resilience.

CHAPTER 9

THE PROBLEM-SOLVING TOOLBOX: FINDING SOLUTIONS WITH CBT

Welcome back, my brilliant buddies! In the last chapter, we had a blast exploring the colorful world of emotions and learning how to be a feelings-friendly superstar. Now, get ready to put on your thinking caps and dive into the exciting realm of problem-solving!

Life is full of all sorts of challenges, big and small. Maybe you're dealing with a tricky math homework problem, a disagreement with a friend, or a tough decision about what to do after school. Whatever the case may be, having a handy set of problem-solving tools can make a world of difference.

That's where Cognitive Behavioral Therapy (CBT) comes in! CBT is like a superhero utility belt for your brain, packed with powerful strategies for tackling any obstacle that comes your way. And the best part? You already have all the tools you need, right inside your amazing mind!

So, what exactly is CBT? It's a fancy way of saying that our thoughts, feelings, and actions are all connected, like pieces of a puzzle. When we learn how to change one piece (like our thoughts), it can have a positive impact on the other pieces too (like our feelings and actions).

Think of it like this: imagine you're building a Lego castle, but you keep running into problems. Maybe the pieces aren't fitting together right, or the castle keeps falling over. You could get frustrated and give up, or you could take a step back, look at the instructions, and try some new strategies.

That's what CBT is all about – learning how to look at problems in a new way, challenge unhelpful thoughts, and find creative solutions. And just like Lego, the more you practice, the better you'll get at building strong, stable structures (or in this case, a strong, resilient mind!).

So, are you ready to open up your problem-solving toolbox? Let's dive in and explore some of the most powerful tools CBT has to offer!

1 The Thought Detective One of the key principles of CBT is that our thoughts have a big impact on how we feel and what we do. But sometimes, our thoughts can be sneaky and unhelpful, like little gremlins running around in our heads. That's where the Thought Detective comes in! This tool is all about putting on your detective hat and investigating your thoughts with curiosity and kindness. For example, let's say you're feeling really nervous about an upcoming presentation at school. Your thought gremlins might be saying things like, "I'm going to mess up and everyone will laugh at me!" or "I'm not good enough to do this." But when you put on your Thought Detective hat, you can start to question those thoughts. You might ask yourself, "Is this thought really true? What evidence do I have to support it?" or "Is this thought helping me or hurting me?" By investigating your thoughts, you can start to see them for what they really are – just thoughts, not facts. And that can help you feel more in control and less stuck in worry or self-doubt.

2 The Perspective Glasses Another helpful CBT tool is the Perspective Glasses. This tool is all about learning to look at problems from different angles, just like trying on a bunch of different pairs of glasses. For example, let's say you're having a disagreement with a friend. You might be feeling really hurt and angry, and your perspective might be something like, "They're being so mean and unfair to me!" But when you put on your Perspective Glasses, you can start to see the situation from other points of view. You might ask yourself, "How might my friend be feeling right now? What might be going on in their life that I don't know about?" or "Is there a way we could both get our needs met in this situation?" By looking at problems from different perspectives, you can start to find more creative and compassionate solutions. You might realize that there's more to the story than you first thought, or that there are ways to compromise and find a win-win.

3 The Coping Kit Life can be full of all sorts of stressors and challenges, from big life changes to daily hassles. That's where the Coping Kit comes in – it's like a first-aid kit for your mental health! A Coping Kit is a collection of tools and strategies that you can use

to manage stress and take care of yourself. It might include things like:
- Deep breathing exercises
- Positive affirmations or mantras
- Calming visualizations or guided meditations
- A list of people you can reach out to for support
- Fun distractions like puzzles, coloring books, or funny videos
- Self-care activities like taking a bubble bath or going for a nature walk

4 The idea is to have a go-to set of tools that you can pull out whenever you're feeling overwhelmed or stressed. By taking proactive steps to cope with challenges, you can build resilience and feel more in control of your well-being.

5 The Experiment Lab Sometimes, the best way to solve a problem is to test out different solutions and see what works. That's where the Experiment Lab comes in! The Experiment Lab is all about approaching problems like a scientist. You start by making a hypothesis (an educated guess) about what might help, then you design an experiment to test it out. For example, let's say you're struggling to focus on your homework because you keep getting distracted by your phone. Your hypothesis might be, "If I put my phone in another room while I study, I'll be able to concentrate better." To test this hypothesis, you could try studying for 30 minutes with your phone in another room, and see how it goes. If it helps, great! If not, you can try a different experiment, like using a website blocker or studying with a friend to hold you accountable. The key is to approach problems with curiosity and a willingness to try new things. By experimenting with different strategies, you can find what works best for you and your unique brain.

6 The Self-Compassion Superhero Last but not least, one of the most powerful tools in your problem-solving toolbox is self-compassion. This means treating yourself with kindness, understanding, and forgiveness, even (especially!) when you're struggling. Think of self-compassion like a superhero cape that you can wrap around yourself whenever you're feeling down or discouraged. It's a way of saying to yourself, "Hey, this is tough, and I'm doing my best. I'm here for you and I believe in you." For example, let's say you're feeling really frustrated because you keep making mistakes on your math homework. Your inner critic might

be saying things like, "You're so stupid! You'll never be good at math." But when you put on your self-compassion superhero cape, you can start to talk to yourself like a kind and supportive friend. You might say something like, "Math can be really challenging sometimes, and it's okay to make mistakes. You're working hard and learning a lot. I'm proud of you for not giving up!" By practicing self-compassion, you can create a safe and nurturing space for yourself to learn, grow, and problem-solve. You can bounce back from setbacks more easily, and approach challenges with a sense of resilience and self-belief.

Phew, that was a lot of tools to explore! But don't worry – you don't have to be an expert at using them all right away. Like any new skill, problem-solving takes practice and patience.

The good news is, every time you face a challenge or obstacle, you have an opportunity to flex your problem-solving muscles and try out a new tool from your toolbox. And the more you practice, the more confident and capable you'll feel in navigating life's ups and downs.

So, the next time you're feeling stuck or overwhelmed by a problem, remember: you've got this! You have a whole toolbox full of strategies and strengths to help you find a way forward. All you have to do is take a deep breath, put on your thinking cap, and give it your best shot.

And don't forget to celebrate your successes along the way! Every time you use a CBT tool to solve a problem or cope with a challenge, you're growing and learning and becoming a more resilient, resourceful version of yourself. That's something to be really proud of.

So here's to a lifetime of creative problem-solving, mental flexibility, and brave, bold thinking! May you always remember that you have the power to face any obstacle with curiosity, compassion, and   a   can-do   spirit.

CHAPTER 10

MINDFULNESS THROUGH ART AND CREATIVITY: EXPRESSING YOURSELF AND FINDING INNER PEACE

Hello, my amazing artistic friends! In the last chapter, we explored the exciting world of problem-solving and discovered some fantastic tools from Cognitive Behavioral Therapy (CBT) to help us tackle any challenge that comes our way. Now, get ready to unleash your inner artist and dive into the colorful realm of mindfulness through art and creativity!

Have you ever lost track of time while drawing, painting, or making something with your hands? Maybe you were so focused on your project that the rest of the world seemed to fade away, and you felt a sense of calm and joy wash over you. That's the magic of mindfulness through art!

Mindfulness is all about paying attention to the present moment with curiosity and kindness. It's about noticing your thoughts, feelings, and sensations without judging them, and learning to be more present and aware in your daily life. And guess what? Art and creativity are some of the most powerful tools we have for practicing mindfulness!

When we engage in creative activities, we tap into a different part of our brain – the part that's all about imagination, intuition, and self-expression. We let go of our worries and distractions, and we allow ourselves to get lost in the flow of making something new. It's like taking a mini-vacation for our minds, and coming back feeling refreshed and inspired.

But the benefits of mindfulness through art go way beyond just feeling good in the moment. Research shows that engaging in creative activities can actually change our brains in positive ways, helping us become more resilient, adaptable, and emotionally intelligent.

For example, when we draw or paint, we practice paying close attention to details and using our observational skills. This can help us become more mindful and present in other areas of our lives, like when we're having a conversation with a friend or trying to solve a problem.

When we write stories or poetry, we tap into our emotions and learn to express ourselves in new ways. This can help us become more self-aware and empathetic, and can even boost our confidence and self-esteem.

And when we make music or dance, we connect with our bodies and our senses in a powerful way. We learn to listen deeply, to move with intention and grace, and to let go of self-judgment and perfectionism.

So, are you ready to explore the wonderful world of mindfulness through art? Let's dive in and discover some fun and creative ways to express yourself and find inner peace!

1 Mindful Drawing One of the simplest and most accessible ways to practice mindfulness through art is through drawing. You don't need any fancy materials or skills – just a piece of paper, a pencil, and an open mind! Here's how to do it:

• Find a quiet, comfortable place where you won't be disturbed.

• Take a few deep breaths and let yourself settle into the present moment.

• Choose an object to draw – it could be something in front of you, like a flower or a cup, or something from your imagination.

• As you draw, focus your attention on the lines, shapes, and textures you're creating. Notice the feel of the pencil in your hand, the sound of the pencil on the paper, and the sensations in your body as you work.

• If your mind starts to wander or you get caught up in judging your drawing, gently bring your attention back to the present moment and the act of creating.

• When you're finished, take a moment to appreciate your creation, without worrying about whether it's "good" or "bad." Remember, the process is more important than the product!

2 By practicing mindful drawing regularly, you can train your brain to be more present, focused, and aware. You might start to

notice details you never saw before, or find new ways of seeing the world around you.

3 Intuitive Painting Another fun way to practice mindfulness through art is through intuitive painting. This is all about letting go of expectations and allowing yourself to be guided by your intuition and emotions. Here's how to do it:

• Set up your painting space with a variety of colors, brushes, and paper or canvas.

• Take a few deep breaths and check in with yourself. Notice any emotions or sensations that are present, without judging them.

• Choose colors that resonate with your current emotional state. Don't think too much about it – just go with your gut!

• As you paint, let your hand move freely across the page. Don't worry about creating a specific image or making it look "good." Just let the colors and shapes emerge naturally.

• If you find yourself getting caught up in thoughts or judgments, gently bring your attention back to the sensations of painting – the feel of the brush in your hand, the smell of the paint, the colors and textures on the page.

• When you're finished, take a step back and observe your painting with curiosity. What do you notice? What feelings or insights emerge?

4 Intuitive painting can be a powerful way to process emotions, express yourself, and tap into your inner wisdom. By letting go of expectations and allowing yourself to be guided by your intuition, you can learn to trust yourself more deeply and find new ways of seeing the world.

5 Mindful Photography You don't have to be a professional photographer to practice mindfulness through photography! All you need is a camera (even a phone camera will do) and a willingness to see the world with fresh eyes. Here's how to do it:

• Choose a place to take a mindful photo walk. It could be a park, a city street, or even your own backyard.

• As you walk, pay attention to your surroundings with all your senses. Notice the colors, shapes, textures, and sounds around you.

• When something catches your eye, pause and take a closer look. What drew you to this particular scene or object? What details do you notice when you look more closely?

• Take a photo of what you see, focusing on composition, lighting, and perspective. Try to capture the essence of what you're experiencing in the moment.

• After you take the photo, take a moment to appreciate it. Notice how it makes you feel, and what insights or memories it evokes.

• Repeat the process as you continue your walk, allowing yourself to be surprised and delighted by the world around you.

6 Mindful photography can help us cultivate a sense of wonder and appreciation for the beauty in everyday life. By learning to see the world through a lens of curiosity and presence, we can find moments of joy and peace wherever we go.

7 Creative Writing Writing is another powerful tool for practicing mindfulness and self-expression. Whether you're journaling, writing poetry, or crafting a story, the act of putting words on the page can help you process your thoughts and feelings, and tap into your creativity. Here are some ideas for mindful writing:

• Set aside some quiet time each day for free-writing. This means writing continuously for a set period of time (say, 10-15 minutes), without worrying about grammar, spelling, or making sense. Just let the words flow onto the page, and see what emerges.

• Try writing from a prompt, like a quote, a question, or a random word. Use the prompt as a starting point, and let your mind wander wherever it wants to go.

• Write a letter to your younger self, offering wisdom, encouragement, and compassion. What would you want that younger version of you to know?

• Keep a gratitude journal, where you write down three things you're grateful for each day. This can help shift your focus to the positive and cultivate a sense of abundance and joy.

• Write a story or poem that expresses a challenging emotion, like anger, fear, or sadness. Use metaphor, imagery, and sensory details to bring the emotion to life on the page.

8 By engaging in mindful writing, we can learn to be more honest and authentic with ourselves, and find new ways of making sense of our experiences. We can also tap into our imagination and creativity, and discover new possibilities for our lives.

9 Musical Expression Music is a universal language that has the power to touch our hearts and souls. Whether you're playing an instrument, singing, or simply listening to your favorite songs, music

can be a powerful tool for practicing mindfulness and self-expression. Here are some ideas for mindful musical expression:

• Choose an instrument that you love (or have always wanted to learn), and set aside time each day to practice. Focus on the sensations of playing – the feel of the instrument in your hands, the vibrations of the sound, the rhythm and flow of the music.

• Sing along to your favorite songs, paying attention to the lyrics and the emotions they evoke. Notice how singing makes you feel in your body and your heart.

• Create a playlist of songs that inspire and uplift you. Listen to the playlist when you need a boost of energy or motivation, or when you want to shift your mood.

• Try writing your own song, even if you've never done it before. Start with a simple melody or chord progression, and let the words and emotions flow from there.

• Attend a live music performance, and allow yourself to be fully present in the moment. Notice the energy of the crowd, the skill of the musicians, and the way the music moves you.

10 By engaging in mindful musical expression, we can tap into a deep well of emotion and creativity. We can also learn to be more present and attuned to the world around us, and find new ways of connecting with ourselves and others.

As you can see, there are so many wonderful ways to practice mindfulness through art and creativity! The key is to approach the process with curiosity, openness, and a willingness to let go of perfection and judgment.

Remember, you don't have to be a professional artist or musician to benefit from these practices. The most important thing is to find activities that resonate with you, and that allow you to express yourself in authentic and meaningful ways.

And don't be afraid to experiment and try new things! You might discover a hidden talent or passion that you never knew you had, or find a new way of seeing the world that transforms your perspective.

So go ahead – pick up a paintbrush, a camera, a pen, or an instrument, and let your creativity flow! Allow yourself to get lost in the process, and see what amazing insights and experiences emerge.

And remember, mindfulness is a practice, not a destination. There will be days when it feels easy and natural, and days when it feels challenging and frustrating. That's all part of the journey, and every moment is an opportunity to learn and grow.

So be patient and kind with yourself, and trust in the power of mindfulness and creativity to guide you towards greater peace, joy, and   self-discovery.

CHAPTER 11

THE GRATITUDE TREASURE HUNT: DISCOVERING THE GOOD IN LIFE

Welcome back, my fantastic friends! In the last chapter, we explored the magical world of mindfulness through art and creativity. We discovered how expressing ourselves through drawing, painting, photography, writing, and music can help us find inner peace and tap into our unique voices. Now, get ready to embark on an exciting new adventure – The Gratitude Treasure Hunt!

What is gratitude, you might ask? Gratitude is all about noticing and appreciating the good things in life, big and small. It's about focusing on what we have, rather than what we lack, and recognizing the abundance of blessings that surround us every day.

But why is gratitude so important? Well, research shows that practicing gratitude can have a powerful positive impact on our mental health and well-being. When we regularly take time to appreciate the good in our lives, we experience more positive emotions, feel more connected to others, and even sleep better at night!

Think of gratitude like a magic magnifying glass that helps us see the world in a whole new light. Instead of getting caught up in worries, complaints, or comparisons, gratitude helps us focus on the beauty, kindness, and wonder that are always present, even in the midst of challenges.

And the best part? Gratitude is a skill that anyone can learn and practice, no matter how old you are or what your life circumstances may be. All it takes is a little bit of intention, attention, and creativity.

So, are you ready to join me on The Gratitude Treasure Hunt? Get ready to discover hidden gems of joy, appreciation, and positive perspective, and learn how to cultivate an attitude of gratitude that will serve you for a lifetime!

1 The Gratitude Journal One of the simplest and most effective ways to practice gratitude is by keeping a gratitude journal. This is a special notebook or diary where you write down things you're thankful for each day. Here's how to do it:

• Find a notebook or journal that you love, and keep it by your bed or in your backpack.

• At the end of each day, take a few minutes to reflect on your experiences and jot down three things you're grateful for.

• Your gratitude entries can be big or small, specific or general. You might write about a delicious meal, a kind word from a friend, a beautiful sunset, or a new skill you learned.

• As you write, take a moment to really feel the emotion of gratitude in your body. Notice how it feels in your heart, your belly, your face.

• If you miss a day or two, don't worry! Just pick up where you left off and keep going.

2 Over time, as you fill your journal with expressions of gratitude, you'll start to notice a shift in your perspective. You'll become more attuned to the good things in life, and more resilient in the face of challenges. You might even start to see opportunities for gratitude in unexpected places!

3 The Gratitude Scavenger Hunt Another fun way to practice gratitude is by going on a Gratitude Scavenger Hunt. This is where you intentionally look for things to appreciate in your environment, like a treasure hunter seeking hidden gems. Here's how to do it:

• Choose a location for your scavenger hunt. It could be your home, your school, your neighborhood, or even a local park.

• Make a list of things to look for on your hunt. Your list might include things like:

• Something that makes you smile
• Something that reminds you of a happy memory
• Something that you can see, hear, smell, taste, and touch
• Something that someone did for you recently
• Something that you're proud of
• As you go about your day, keep your list in mind and actively look for things that fit each category.

• When you find something to appreciate, take a moment to really savor it. Notice how it makes you feel, and maybe even snap a photo or write a note about it.

• At the end of your hunt, take a few minutes to reflect on your experiences. What did you discover? How did it feel to actively seek out things to appreciate?

4 The Gratitude Scavenger Hunt is a great way to train your brain to notice and appreciate the good things in life, even when they're not immediately obvious. By actively seeking out things to be grateful for, you're strengthening your gratitude muscle and cultivating a more positive outlook on life.

5 The Gratitude Letter One of the most powerful ways to express gratitude is by writing a letter to someone who has made a positive impact on your life. This could be a family member, a friend, a teacher, or even a stranger who showed you kindness. Here's how to do it:

• Choose someone to write to who you feel grateful for. It could be someone who has always been there for you, or someone who recently did something nice for you.

• Take a few minutes to reflect on why you're grateful for this person. What specific things have they done or said that made a difference in your life?

• Write a letter expressing your gratitude. Be specific about what you appreciate, and how it has impacted you. Share a memory or story that illustrates your point.

• As you write, let yourself really feel the emotion of gratitude. Notice how it feels in your body and your heart.

• When you're finished, you can choose to send the letter, give it to the person in person, or simply keep it as a reminder of your gratitude.

6 The Gratitude Letter is a powerful way to deepen your own experience of gratitude, while also spreading positivity and appreciation to others. By taking the time to express your thanks in writing, you're not only boosting your own well-being, but also strengthening your relationships and connections with the people who matter most.

7 The Gratitude Meditation Meditation is a wonderful way to cultivate mindfulness and inner peace, and it can also be a powerful tool for practicing gratitude. By taking a few minutes each day to sit

in silence and focus on the things you're thankful for, you can deepen your experience of gratitude and train your brain to notice the good in life. Here's how to do it:

• Find a quiet, comfortable place to sit where you won't be disturbed.

• Close your eyes and take a few deep breaths, letting yourself settle into the present moment.

• Bring to mind something or someone you're grateful for. It could be a person, a place, an experience, or even a simple pleasure like a warm cup of tea.

• As you hold this thing in your mind, notice how it makes you feel. What sensations do you notice in your body? What emotions arise?

• If your mind starts to wander, gently bring your attention back to your chosen object of gratitude.

• You can repeat this process with different things you're grateful for, or simply rest your attention on one thing for the duration of your meditation.

• When you're ready to finish, take a few deep breaths and slowly open your eyes.

8 The Gratitude Meditation is a simple but powerful way to connect with feelings of appreciation and abundance. By taking a few minutes each day to focus on the good in your life, you're training your brain to see the world through a lens of gratitude and positivity.

9 The Gratitude Collage If you're a visual person, you might enjoy creating a Gratitude Collage – a colorful, creative representation of the things you're thankful for. This is a fun and engaging way to practice gratitude that allows you to express yourself through art and imagery. Here's how to do it:

• Gather your materials. You'll need some magazines, scissors, glue, and a piece of poster board or cardboard.

• Take a few minutes to reflect on the things you're grateful for. Make a list if it helps you keep track.

• Flip through your magazines and cut out images, words, and phrases that represent the things on your gratitude list. You can also draw or write your own additions.

• Arrange your cutouts on your poster board in a way that feels meaningful and visually appealing to you. You might group similar items together, or create a collage that tells a story.

• As you work, take time to really appreciate each item and reflect on why it matters to you.

• When you're finished, hang your Gratitude Collage somewhere you'll see it often, like your bedroom wall or your locker at school.

10 The Gratitude Collage is a wonderful way to create a tangible reminder of the good things in your life. By expressing your gratitude through art and imagery, you're engaging your creativity and your senses, and creating a powerful visual cue to help you stay focused on positivity and appreciation.

As you can see, there are so many fun and meaningful ways to practice gratitude! Whether you prefer writing, meditating, or making art, the key is to find a practice that resonates with you and that you can stick with over time.

Remember, gratitude isn't about ignoring or denying the challenges and difficulties in life. It's about intentionally shifting your focus to the things that are going right, and cultivating a sense of appreciation and abundance even in the midst of hardship.

And the more you practice gratitude, the more natural and automatic it will become. Over time, you'll start to notice little moments of joy and beauty throughout your day that you might have overlooked before. You'll become more resilient in the face of setbacks and challenges, and more connected to the people and experiences that matter most.

So go ahead – grab your journal, your camera, your scissors and glue, and start your own Gratitude Treasure Hunt! Let yourself be surprised and delighted by the everyday magic that surrounds you, and watch as your life becomes infused with more positivity, purpose, and joy.

And don't forget to share your gratitude with others, too! By expressing your appreciation and thanks to the people in your life, you're not only boosting your own well-being, but also spreading ripples of kindness and connection that can transform your relationships and your community.

So here's to a lifetime of gratitude, appreciation, and joy! May you always remember to look for the good, count your blessings, and treasure the ordinary miracles that make life so rich and wonderful.

CHAPTER 12

THE MINDFULNESS AND CBT ADVENTURE CONTINUES: PUTTING IT ALL TOGETHER

Welcome to the final chapter of our incredible journey, my amazing friends! Throughout this book, we've explored the wondrous worlds of mindfulness and Cognitive Behavioral Therapy (CBT), and discovered a treasure trove of tools and strategies for nurturing our mental health and well-being.

We started by learning about the magic of a happy mind, and how CBT and mindfulness can help us navigate life's ups and downs with greater ease and resilience. We discovered the power of the thought-feeling connection, and how becoming friends with our minds can transform our experiences and relationships.

We unleashed the superpower of positive thinking, and learned how to challenge negative thoughts and cultivate a more optimistic outlook. We embarked on mindful breathing adventures, and discovered how focusing on the present moment can bring us greater calm and clarity.

We explored the magic of everyday mindfulness, and learned how to find joy and wonder in the ordinary moments of life. We faced our fears and worries with the help of our CBT toolbox, and discovered that we are braver and stronger than we ever imagined.

We learned to treat ourselves with kindness and compassion, and discovered the transformative power of self-love and self-care. We made friends with our feelings, and learned how to embrace and express our emotions in healthy ways.

We became problem-solving superheroes, and learned how to use CBT strategies to tackle any challenge that comes our way. We expressed ourselves through art and creativity, and discovered the healing power of mindfulness and self-expression.

And finally, we embarked on a gratitude treasure hunt, and learned how to cultivate an attitude of appreciation and abundance that can transform our lives and relationships.

Phew, what an incredible journey it's been! But the adventure doesn't stop here. In fact, the real magic happens when we take all these tools and strategies and start applying them in our daily lives.

So, how can we put it all together and make mindfulness and CBT a regular part of our routines? Here are some ideas to get you started:

1 Make mindfulness a daily habit. Just like brushing your teeth or getting dressed, make mindfulness a non-negotiable part of your daily routine. Set aside a few minutes each day to practice mindful breathing, meditation, or any other mindfulness activity that resonates with you. For example, you might start your day with a few minutes of mindful stretching or yoga, or take a mindful walk during your lunch break. You might end your day with a gratitude journal entry or a body scan meditation. The key is to find a practice that works for you and stick with it, even when life gets busy or stressful.

2 Use CBT tools in real-time. CBT isn't just something you do in a therapist's office or during a designated "therapy time." It's a set of tools and strategies that you can use anytime, anywhere, to help you manage your thoughts and emotions and navigate challenges. For example, when you notice yourself getting caught up in negative thoughts or worries, you can use your CBT tools to challenge and reframe those thoughts. You might ask yourself, "Is this thought really true? What evidence do I have to support it? Is there another way of looking at this situation?" Or when you're facing a difficult problem or decision, you can use your problem-solving skills to break it down into smaller, manageable steps and brainstorm creative solutions. You might make a pros and cons list, or do a cost-benefit analysis to help you weigh your options.

3 Surround yourself with support. Mindfulness and CBT are powerful tools, but they're not meant to be used in isolation. In fact, one of the most important aspects of mental health and well-being is having a strong support system of people who love and care for you. So, don't be afraid to reach out for help and support when you need it. Talk to a trusted friend or family member about what you're going through, and ask for their encouragement and guidance. Consider

joining a support group or seeing a therapist who can help you work through specific challenges or goals. And don't forget to be a source of support for others, too! By sharing your own experiences and insights, and offering a listening ear and a helping hand to those in need, you're not only strengthening your own resilience and compassion, but also making a positive difference in the world around you.

4 Celebrate your progress and growth. As you continue on your mindfulness and CBT journey, it's important to take time to acknowledge and celebrate your progress and growth. It's easy to get caught up in what we haven't achieved or what we still struggle with, but true success is measured by how far we've come, not just where we end up. So, make a habit of reflecting on your experiences and accomplishments, and give yourself credit for the hard work and courage it takes to show up for yourself every day. Keep a journal of your insights and breakthroughs, or create a vision board that represents your hopes and dreams for the future. And when you face setbacks or challenges (which are inevitable on any journey of growth), remember to be kind and compassionate with yourself. Treat yourself with the same love and understanding you would offer to a dear friend, and trust that every stumble is an opportunity to learn and grow.

As we come to the end of this book, I want to leave you with a few final thoughts and words of encouragement.

First, remember that mindfulness and CBT are not a destination, but a journey. There's no such thing as being "done" with these practices, because there's always more to learn and discover about ourselves and the world around us. Embrace the ongoing nature of this work, and trust that every step you take is bringing you closer to a life of greater peace, purpose, and joy.

Second, don't be afraid to make these practices your own. Mindfulness and CBT are not one-size-fits-all approaches, and what works for one person may not work for another. Experiment with different tools and strategies, and find the ones that resonate most deeply with your unique personality, values, and goals. The more you can tailor these practices to your individual needs and preferences, the more sustainable and effective they'll be in the long run.

And finally, never underestimate the power of your own inner wisdom and strength. You are the expert on your own life, and you have within you all the resources and resilience you need to thrive and flourish. Trust your instincts, follow your heart, and know that you are capable of amazing things.

So here's to a lifetime of mindfulness, self-discovery, and growth! May you always remember to breathe deeply, think positively, and treat yourself with kindness and compassion. May you face your fears with courage and curiosity, and may you find joy and wonder in the everyday moments of life.

And above all, may you always know that you are loved, valued, and deserving of every good thing life has to offer. Keep shining your light, my amazing friends, and know that the world is a brighter place because of you!

Summary and Conclusion:

In this book, we've explored the incredible world of mindfulness and Cognitive Behavioral Therapy, and discovered a wealth of tools and strategies for nurturing our mental health and well-being.

We've learned about the power of the thought-feeling connection, and how becoming friends with our minds can transform our experiences and relationships. We've unleashed the superpower of positive thinking, and learned how to challenge negative thoughts and cultivate a more optimistic outlook.

We've embarked on mindful breathing adventures, and discovered the magic of everyday mindfulness. We've faced our fears and worries with the help of our CBT toolbox, and learned to treat ourselves with kindness and compassion.

We've become problem-solving superheroes, and expressed ourselves through art and creativity. And we've embarked on a gratitude treasure hunt, learning to cultivate an attitude of appreciation and abundance that can transform our lives and relationships.

But the real magic happens when we take all these tools and strategies and start applying them in our daily lives. By making mindfulness a daily habit, using CBT tools in real-time, surrounding ourselves with support, and celebrating our progress and growth, we can create a life of greater peace, purpose, and joy.

Remember, mindfulness and CBT are not a destination, but a journey. Embrace the ongoing nature of this work, and trust that every step you take is bringing you closer to your best self. Don't be afraid to make these practices your own, and tailor them to your unique needs and preferences.

And above all, never underestimate the power of your own inner wisdom and strength. You have within you all the resources and resilience you need to thrive and flourish. Trust yourself, follow your heart, and know that you are capable of amazing things.

So here's to a lifetime of mindfulness, self-discovery, and growth! May you always remember to breathe deeply, think positively, and treat yourself with kindness and compassion. May you shine your light brightly, and know that the world is a better place because of you.

Thank you for joining me on this incredible journey, my amazing friends. It's been an honor and a privilege to share these practices and insights with you, and I hope they'll continue to inspire and support you on your path to a happy, healthy mind.

Keep shining, keep growing, and keep embracing the magic of mindfulness and CBT! The adventure continues, and I can't wait to see where it takes you next.

With love, gratitude, and endless faith in your incredible potential,

Your mindfulness and CBT guide.